A MIDSUMMER NIGHT'S DREAM

THE GRAPHIC NOVEL
William Shakespeare

Based on a script by John McDonald

NATIONAL GEOGRAPHIC LEARNING | HEINLE CENGAGE Learning

Australia • Brazil • Japan • Korea • Mexico • Singapore • Spain • United Kingdom • United States

A Midsummer Night's Dream:
The Graphic Novel
William Shakespeare

Publisher: Sherrise Roehr

Editor in Chief: Clive Bryant

Associate Development Editor:
  Cécile Engeln

Director of U.S. Marketing:
  Jim McDonough

Assistant Marketing Manager:
  Jide Iruka

Director of Content Production:
  Michael Burggren

Associate Content Project
  Manager: Mark Rzeszutek

Print Buyer: Sue Spencer

Character Design and Artwork:
  Jason Cardy and Kat
  Nicholson

Lettering: Jim Campbell

Associate Editor: Joe Sutliff
  Sanders

Design and Layout: Jenny
  Placentino

ISBN-13: 978-1-111-83845-4

ISBN-10: 1-111-83845-3

National Geographic Learning
20 Channel Center Street
Boston, MA 02210
USA

Cengage Learning is a leading provider of customized learning solutions with office locations around the globe, including Singapore, the United Kingdom, Australia, Mexico, Brazil, and Japan.

Cengage Learning products are represented in Canada by Nelson Education, Ltd.

Visit National Geographic Learning online at **elt.heinle.com**

Visit our corporate website at **www.cengage.com**

Printed in China
5 6 7 8 18 17 16 15

Contents

Characters

Theseus
Duke of Athens

Hippolyta
Queen of the Amazons

Egeus
Hermia's Father

Hermia
*Egeus's Daughter,
in love with Lysander*

Lysander
In love with Hermia

Peter Quince
An actor

Nick Bottom
An actor

Nick Bottom
As a donkey

Snug
An actor

Robin Starveling
An actor

Tom Snout
An actor

Oberon
King of the Fairies

Titania
Queen of the Fairies

Helena
In love with Demetrius

Demetrius
In love with Hermia

Puck (or Robin Goodfellow)
An elf, Oberon's jester

Francis
An actor

Philostrate
Master of the Revels

Peaseblossom, Cobweb, Moth and Mustardseed
Fairies

5

A
MIDSUMMER
NIGHT'S
DREAM

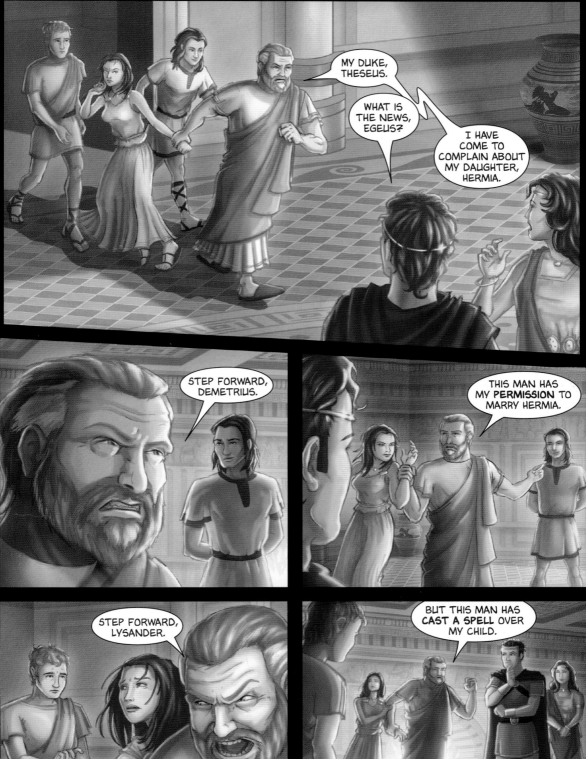

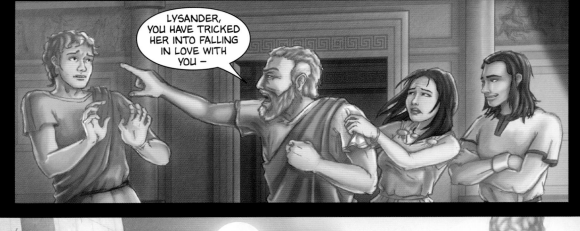

11

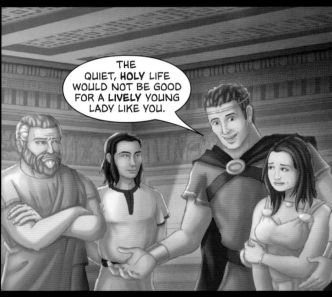

ATHENS – A ROOM IN QUINCE'S HOUSE

ARE ALL THE ACTORS HERE?

CALL ALL THE NAMES ONE BY ONE.

THIS IS A LIST OF THE ACTORS WHO ARE GOING TO **PERFORM** FOR THE DUKE'S WEDDING.

FIRST, TELL US WHAT THE PLAY IS ABOUT. THEN READ THE NAMES.

IT IS CALLED, "THE VERY TRAGIC COMEDY OF PYRAMUS AND THISBE."

THAT IS A GREAT PLAY – VERY FUNNY. READ THE NAMES OF THE ACTORS.

GENTLEMEN, SPREAD OUT.

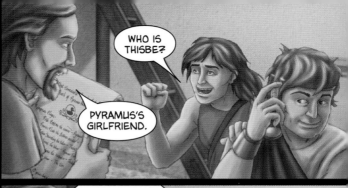

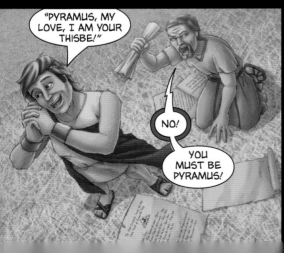

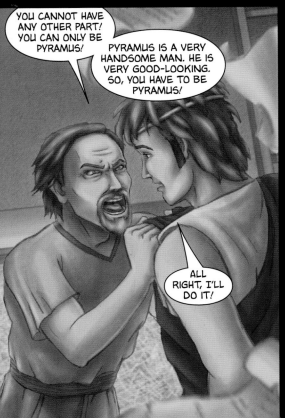

29

33

34

35

I KNOW WHERE TITANIA LIKES TO SLEEP.

I WILL SQUEEZE THE JUICE OF THIS FLOWER ONTO HER *EYELIDS* AND FILL HER MIND WITH STRANGE THOUGHTS.

THERE IS A RUDE YOUNG MAN IN THE FOREST. HE IS *REJECTING* THE LOVE OF A SWEET GIRL.

FIND HIM AND PUT THE JUICE ON HIS *EYELIDS* ALSO. MAKE SURE THIS GIRL IS THE FIRST THING HE SEES WHEN HE WAKES UP.

THE MAN IS WEARING *ATHENIAN* CLOTHES.

DO IT VERY CAREFULLY! MAKE HIM LOVE HER MORE THAN SHE LOVES HIM.

THEN WE WILL MEET WHEN THE SUN STARTS TO RISE.

I WILL DO IT, MY LORD.

43

47

53

WE NEED A CALENDAR!

WE ARE GOING TO NEED **MOONLIGHT** FOR THE PLAY. PYRAMUS AND THISBE MET BY **MOONLIGHT.**

WILL THE MOON BE SHINING THE NIGHT OF OUR PLAY?

YES, THE MOON WILL SHINE THAT NIGHT.

THEN JUST LEAVE A WINDOW OPEN, AND THE MOON CAN SHINE THROUGH IT.

IT MIGHT BE BETTER IF SOMEONE COMES **ONSTAGE,** DRESSED AS THE MOON.

AND WE WILL NEED A WALL. PYRAMUS AND THISBE SPOKE THROUGH A HOLE IN A WALL.

WE CAN'T BRING A WALL **ONSTAGE.**

SOMEONE CAN CARRY STONES AND PRETEND HE'S A WALL.

HE CAN HOLD HIS FINGERS LIKE THIS BECAUSE PYRAMUS AND THISBE SPOKE THROUGH A HOLE IN THE WALL.

THAT MIGHT WORK.

ANOTHER PART OF THE FOREST

I WONDER IF TITANIA IS AWAKE –

– AND I WONDER WHAT AWFUL THING SHE SAW AND FELL IN LOVE WITH.

HERE COMES PUCK.

WELL? WHAT IS HAPPENING?

TITANIA IS IN LOVE WITH A *MONSTER.*

A GROUP OF ACTORS, NOT THE SMARTEST BUNCH, WHO WORK IN **ATHENS** FOR THEIR LUNCH,

WERE TRYING TO **REHEARSE** A PLAY, CLOSE TO WHERE TITANIA LAY.

THE ONE MOST STUPID OF THEM ALL, INTO A BUSH DID CRAWL;

AND WHILE HE WAS IN THERE, I GAVE HIM A DONKEY HEAD TO WEAR.

WHEN THE OTHERS SAW HIS *DISGUISE*, THEY REALLY COULDN'T BELIEVE THEIR EYES!

THEY SHOUTED FOR HELP AND RAN LIKE GEESE, WHILE HE TRIED HARD TO KEEP THE PEACE.

THEY RAN THROUGH THE FOREST, SCARED OUT OF THEIR WITS, IGNORING THE THORNS THAT SCRATCHED THEM TO BITS.

THEN TITANIA WOKE AND LOOKED OUT FROM HER BED, AND FELL IN LOVE WITH THE DONKEY HEAD.

70

HERE COMES THE ONE YOU LOVE.

I COULDN'T SEE — IT WAS TOO DARK —

— SO I FOLLOWED YOUR VOICES.

THAT'S HOW I WAS ABLE TO FIND YOU, LYSANDER.

WHY DID YOU LEAVE ME ALONE LIKE THAT?

I COULDN'T STAY. LOVE MADE ME GO.

WHAT KIND OF LOVE WOULD MAKE YOU LEAVE ME?

MY LOVE —

— FOR HELENA. I LOVE HER NOW. YOU SHOULDN'T HAVE FOLLOWED ME. I DON'T LIKE YOU ANYMORE.

YOU DON'T MEAN THAT.

YOU ARE IN ON THE JOKE, TOO!

HOW CAN YOU BE SO HURTFUL, HERMIA, TEASING ME WITH THEM?

79

WHEN THEY WAKE UP, ALL WILL BE FINE.

NOW, LET'S GO TO TITANIA AND MAKE THAT BOY MINE!

THEN I WILL REMOVE THE *SPELL* – SHE WON'T LOVE THE DONKEY, AND ALL WILL BE WELL.

WE'LL HAVE TO ACT FAST. THE NIGHT HAS NEARLY PASSED.

GHOSTS AND *SPIRITS* THAT WALK AT NIGHT HAVE TO HIDE THEMSELVES FROM THE LIGHT.

BUT WE ARE *FAIRIES* – WE LIVE DIFFERENT LIVES. WE DON'T HAVE TO HIDE WHEN MORNING ARRIVES.

BUT HURRY, HURRY, WITHOUT DELAY – WE COULD FIX ALL OF THIS BEFORE IT'S DAY.

AAAARGH

85

AAAAAH

I WISH IT WAS MORNING, SO I COULD FIND MY WAY BACK TO ATHENS.

I'LL SLEEP HERE FOR A WHILE. MAYBE I'LL FEEL BETTER WHEN I WAKE UP.

ONLY THREE? I NEED ONE MORE. TWO MEN AND TWO WOMEN MAKE FOUR.

HERE SHE COMES, CONFUSED AND SAD. *CUPID* SHOULDN'T MAKE GIRLS FEEL SO BAD.

I'M TIRED, SCRATCHED, AND WET. I REALLY CAN'T GO ON.

I'LL REST HERE UNTIL THE MORNING. GOD PROTECT LYSANDER IF DEMETRIUS FIGHTS HIM.

89

91

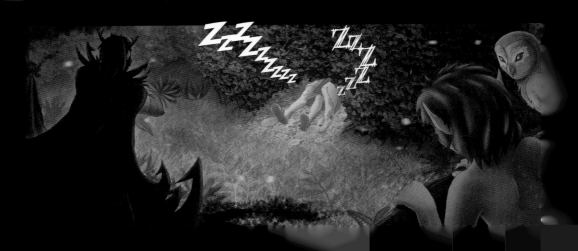

95

=yawn=

GOOD MORNING, FRIENDS. IT ISN'T VALENTINE'S DAY, SO WHAT ARE YOU UP TO?

FORGIVE US, MY LORD.

STAND UP.

WHAT HAPPENED TO THE HATE AND **JEALOUSY** BETWEEN YOU, LYSANDER, AND DEMETRIUS?

I AM STILL CONFUSED, MY LORD. I DON'T KNOW HOW I GOT HERE.

I THINK — YES — I CAME HERE WITH HERMIA.

WE WERE RUNNING AWAY FROM **ATHENS** TOGETHER.

CALL ME WHEN I'M SUPPOSED TO COME OUT. I THINK MY CUE IS "HANDSOME PYRAMUS."

HELLO? PETER QUINCE? FLUTE? SNOUT? STARVELING?

THEY LEFT ME HERE ALL ALONE?

I HAD A STRANGE DREAM.

I WOULD LOOK SO FOOLISH IF I TRIED TO EXPLAIN IT.

I THOUGHT I WAS . . .

I THOUGHT I HAD . . .

I CAN'T DESCRIBE WHAT I THOUGHT I HAD OR WHAT MY DREAM WAS.

I'LL GET PETER QUINCE TO WRITE A SONG ABOUT IT. IT WILL BE CALLED "BOTTOM'S DREAM" BECAUSE IT IS SO DEEP, IT HAS NO BOTTOM.

I'LL SING IT AT THE END OF THE PLAY.

ATHENS – A ROOM IN QUINCE'S HOUSE

IS BOTTOM BACK YET?

NO ONE HAS HEARD FROM HIM.

THE PLAY IS RUINED – WE CAN'T DO IT WITHOUT HIM.

NO ONE CAN BE PYRAMUS LIKE BOTTOM CAN.

HE IS THE MOST TALENTED MAN IN ATHENS!

HIS VOICE IS – WELL – LIKE GRATES.

LIKE THE GREATS, YOU MEAN. HIS VOICE DOESN'T GRATE.

THE DUKE IS LEAVING THE TEMPLE.

TWO OTHER COUPLES WERE ALSO MARRIED.

WE WOULD HAVE MADE A LOT OF MONEY FROM OUR PLAY.

THE DUKE WOULD HAVE PAID BOTTOM FOR PLAYING PYRAMUS. NOW HE WON'T GET THAT MONEY.

Act V, Scene I

ATHENS – OUTSIDE THE PALACE OF THESEUS

THE STORY THESE COUPLES ARE TELLING IS VERY STRANGE, THESEUS.

I DON'T BELIEVE ANY OF THESE **FAIRY TALES.**

LOVERS AND CRAZY PEOPLE HAVE WILD IMAGINATIONS.

CRAZY PEOPLE, **LOVERS,** AND POETS – THEY ARE ALL THE SAME.

THEY IMAGINE THEY SEE THINGS ALL THE TIME.

THEY BELIEVE IN THINGS THAT DON'T EXIST. THEIR MINDS PLAY TRICKS ON THEM.

THEY LIKE TO THINK GOOD THINGS HAPPEN BECAUSE OF SOME **SUPERNATURAL FORCE.**

THEY IMAGINE THEY SEE THINGS IN THE DARK.

BUT THEY ARE ALL SAYING THE SAME STORY – THEY COULDN'T HAVE ALL HAD THE SAME DREAM.

HERE COME THE HAPPY **LOVERS** NOW.

I WISH YOU JOY, MY FRIENDS. MAY JOY AND LOVE ALWAYS LIVE IN YOUR HEARTS.

WE WISH YOU HAPPINESS, MY LORD.

IS THERE ANY **ENTERTAINMENT** FOR US?

WHERE IS PHILOSTRATE?

CALL PHILOSTRATE!

HERE I AM, MIGHTY THESEUS.

117

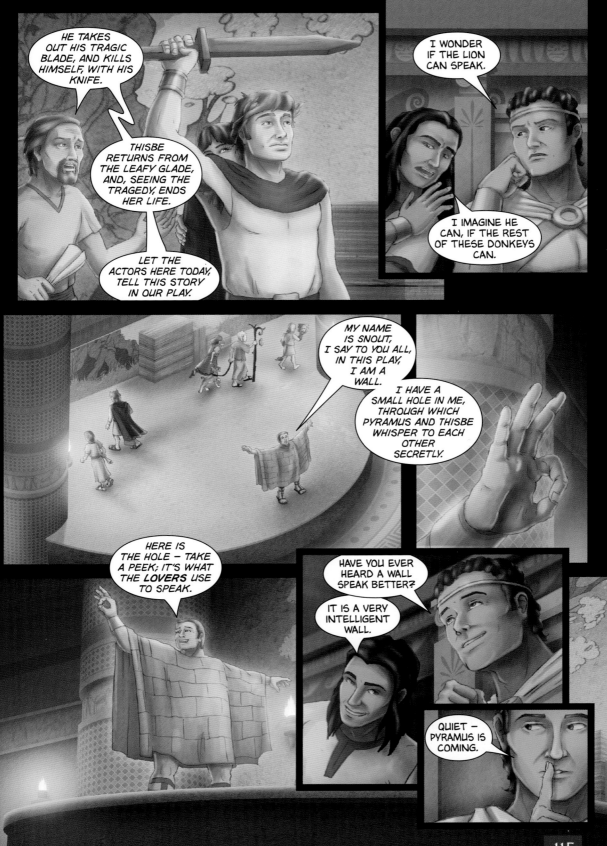

117

clap clap

clap clap clap clap

SO MANY *DIES* FOR ONE PERSON.

NO MORE NOW – HE IS DEAD.

A DOCTOR MIGHT SAVE HIM, SO HE CAN LIVE TO BE A FOOL!

WHY HAS THE MOON GONE BEFORE THISBE HAS COME BACK?

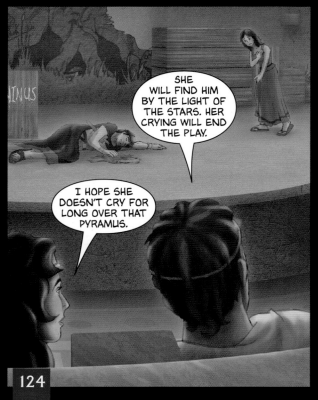

SHE WILL FIND HIM BY THE LIGHT OF THE STARS. HER CRYING WILL END THE PLAY.

I HOPE SHE DOESN'T CRY FOR LONG OVER THAT PYRAMUS.

IT IS HARD TO SAY WHETHER PYRAMUS OR THISBE IS THE BETTER ACTOR.

SHE HAS SEEN HIM.

NOW SHE WILL START TO CRY.

MY LOVE, IN A HEAP! DEAD? OR ASLEEP?
SPEAK TO ME, DEAR; IT'S THE WORST, I FEAR.
YOUR RED NOSE, AND LIPS SO PALE, AND SO IT GOES, YOUR LIFE, SO FRAIL.
OH, POWER ON HIGH, PLEASE HELP ME DIE.
WITH HIM, YOU FOUGHT, AND CUT HIS TIME SHORT.
NOT ANOTHER WORD! I'LL TAKE THIS SWORD.
I MUST DIE!
GOOD-BYE!
GOOD-BYE!

clap

THE MOON AND THE LION WILL BURY THEM.

AND THE WALL, TOO.

clap *clap*

NO, THE WALL HAS BEEN KNOCKED DOWN.

WOULD YOU LIKE TO HEAR THE ENDING SPEECH? OR WATCH US DANCE?

NO SPEECH, PLEASE! NO MORE CAN BE SAID.

IT WOULD HAVE BEEN GREAT IF THE PLAYWRIGHT HAD **HANGED** HIMSELF WITH THISBE'S GARTER.

≈oOOf≈

FORGET ABOUT THE SPEECH — LET'S SEE YOUR DANCE.

IT IS MIDNIGHT — TIME FOR BED. I MIGHT SLEEP IN TOMORROW MORNING, BUT I DON'T MIND. THIS PLAY WAS VERY AMUSING.

WE'LL CONTINUE THESE **CELEBRATIONS** FOR TWO MORE WEEKS!

A MIDSUMMER NIGHT'S DREAM

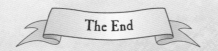

The End

Glossary

A

admirer /ədmaɪərər/ - (admirers) (N) An admirer is a person who likes and respects someone or something.

adore /ədɔr/ - (adores, adoring, adored) (V) If you adore someone, you feel great love and admiration for them.

angel /eɪndʒəl/ - (angels) (N) If you describe someone as an angel, you mean that they seem to be very kind and good.

apply /əplaɪ/ - 1. (applies, applying, applied) (V) If something such as a rule or a remark applies to a person or a situation, it is relevant to them. 2. (applies, applying, applied) (V) If you apply something to a surface, you put it on or rub it into the surface.

approval /əpruvəl/ - (N) If you have a someone's approval, it means they agree to your plan or idea and say that it can happen.

arrow /ærou/ - (arrows) (N) An arrow is a long thin weapon that is sharp and pointed at one end. An arrow is shot from a bow.

Athenian /əθiniɛn/ - 1. (Athenians) (N) An Athenian is a person who is from, or lives in, Athens. 2. (ADJ) Athenian means something that relates to Athens or its people.

Athens /aθənz/ - (N) Athens is the capital of Greece. It is the largest city in Greece.

attract /ətrækt/ - (attracts, attracting, attracted) (V) If someone or something attracts you, they have particular qualities which cause you to like or admire them. When a magnet attracts another magnet, they are pulled toward each other.

audience /ɔdiəns/ - (audiences) (N) The audience of a play, concert, movie, or television program is all the people who are watching or listening to it.

B

background /bækgraʊnd/ - (backgrounds) (N) Your background is the kind of family you come from and the kind of education you have had.

blessing /blɛsɪŋ/ - (blessings) (N) If something is done with your blessing, it is done with your approval and support.

bow - 1. /baʊ/ (bows, bowing, bowed) (V) When you bow to someone, you briefly bend your body toward them as a formal way of greeting them or showing respect. 2. /boʊ/ (bows) (N) A bow is a weapon for shooting arrows that consists of a long piece of curved wood with a string attached to both its ends.

break a promise /breɪk el prɒmɪs/ - (PHRASE) When you break a promise, you don't do something that you told another person you would definitely do.

breed /brid/ - (breeds) (N) A breed of animal is a particular type of it. For example, terriers are a breed of dog.

C

cast /kæst/ - (casts) (N) The cast of a play or movie is all the people who act in it.

cast a spell /kæst ə spɛl/ - (PHRASE) If you cast a spell, you cause or create a situation in which events are controlled by a magical power.

celebration /sɛlɪbreɪʃən/ - (celebrations) (N) A celebration is a joyful party or event to mark some special occasion.

charm /tʃɑrm/ - (charms) (N) A charm is a magical force that may change a person or cause them to act differently.

clan /klæn/ - (clans) (N) A clan is a group which consists of families that are related to each other.

compete /kəmpit/ - (competes, competing, competed) (V) When one person or team competes with another for something, it tries to get that thing for themselves and stop the other from getting it.

convent /kɒnvɛnt/ - (convents) (N) A convent is a building in which a community of nuns lives.

court /kɔrt/ - (courts, courting, courted) (V) If you court something such as publicity or popularity, you try to attract it.

courtesy /kɜrtɪsi/ - (N) Courtesy is politeness, respect, and consideration for others.

coward /kaʊərd/ - (cowards) (N) A coward is someone who is easily frightened and avoids dangerous or difficult situations.

crescent moon /krɛsᵊnt mun/ - (N) A crescent moon is when the moon looks like a thin curve.

crop /krɒp/ - (crops) (N) Crops are plants such as wheat and potatoes that are grown in large quantities for food.

Cupid /kyupəd/ - (N) Cupid is the Roman god of love. He is thought to have a bow and arrow that he uses to make others fall in love.

cut something short /kʌt sʌməɪŋ ʃɔrt/ - (PHRASE) If something is cut short, it is ended sooner than planned.

D

dewdrop /dudrɒp/ - (dewdrops) (N) A dewdrop is a small bit of water that forms on the ground and other surfaces outdoors during the night.

disguise /dɪsgaɪz/ - 1. (disguises) (N) A disguise is something you wear to alter your appearance so that people will not recognize you. 2. (disguises, disguising, disguised) (V) If you disguise yourself, you put on clothes which make you look like someone else or alter your appearance in other ways so that people will not recognize you.

disobey /dɪsəbeɪ/ - (disobeys, disobeying, disobeyed) (V) When someone disobeys a person or an order, they deliberately do not do what they have been told to do.

dove /dʌv/ - (doves) (N) A dove is a bird that looks like a pigeon but is smaller and lighter in color. Doves are often used as a symbol of peace.

dwarf /dwɔrf/ - (dwarfs, dwarves) (N) In children's stories, a dwarf is an imaginary creature that is like a small man. Dwarfs often have magical powers.

E

elf /ɛlf/ - (elves) (N) An elf is a small fairy that often likes to cause trouble.

engaged /ɪngeɪdʒd/ - (ADJ) When two people are engaged, they have agreed to marry each other.

entertainment /ɛntərteɪnmənt/ - (entertainments) (N) Entertainment consists of performances of plays and movies, and activities such as reading and watching television, that give people pleasure.

execute /ɛksɪkyut/ - (executes, executing, executed) (V) To execute someone means to kill them as a punishment.

eyelid /aɪlɪd/ - (eyelids) (N) Your eyelids are the two pieces of skin that cover your eyes when they are closed.

F

fairy /fɛəri/ - (fairies) (N) A fairy is an imaginary creature with magical powers. Fairies are often represented as small people with wings.

fairy ring /fɛəri rɪŋ/ - (fairy rings) (N) A fairy ring is a gathering and dancing spot for fairies.

fairy tale /fɛəri teɪl/ - (fairy tales) (N) A fairy tale is a story for children involving magical events and imaginary creatures.

fault /fɔlt/ - 1. (faults) (N) If a bad or undesirable situation is your fault, you caused it or are responsible for it. 2. (faults) (N) A fault in someone or something is a weakness in them or something that is not perfect.

fog /fɒg/ - (fogs) (N) When there is fog, there are tiny drops of water in the air which form a thick cloud and make it difficult to see things.

frown /fraʊn/ - (frowns, frowning, frowned) (V) When someone frowns, their eyebrows become drawn together because they are annoyed, worried, or puzzled or because they are concentrating.

G

gamekeeper /geɪmkɪpər/ - (gamekeepers) (N) A gamekeeper is in charge of breeding and protecting animals.

grate /greɪt/ - 1. (grates, grating) (N) A grate is a framework of metal bars in a fireplace which holds the wood or coal. 2. (grates, grating, grated) (V) When something grates, it rubs against something else, making a harsh, unpleasant sound.

H

hang /hæŋ/ - (hangs, hanging, hung or hanged) (V) If someone is hanged or if they hang, they are killed by having a rope tied around their neck and the support taken away from under their feet.

I

in on something /ɪn ɒn sʌmθɪŋ/ - (PHRASE) If you are in on something, like a joke, you are participating or have knowledge about what is going on.

introduction /ɪntrədʌkʃən/ - (introductions) (N) The introduction to a book or talk is the part that comes at the beginning and tells you what the rest of the book or talk is about.

invisible /ɪnvɪzɪbəl/ - (ADJ) If something is invisible, you cannot see it, for example, because it is transparent, hidden, or very small.

J

jealous /dʒɛləs/ - (ADJ) If you are jealous of another person's possessions or qualities, you feel angry or bitter because you do not have them.

jealousy /dʒɛləsi/ - (N) Jealousy is the feeling of anger or bitterness that someone has when they wish that they could have the qualities or possessions that another person has.

judgment /dʒʌdʒmənt/ - (judgments) (N) A judgment is an opinion that you have or express after thinking carefully about something.

L

lantern /læntərn/ - (lanterns) (N) A lantern is a lamp in a metal frame with glass sides.

lines /laɪnz/ - (N) An actor's lines are the words they speak in a play or movie.

lively /laɪvli/ - (livelier, liveliest) (ADJ) You can describe someone as lively when they behave in an enthusiastic and cheerful way.

lover /lʌvər/ - (lovers) (N) A lover is a person who is in love.

lovesick /lʌvsɪk/ (lovesickness) (ADJ) If you are lovesick, you are in love and feel weak, unhappy, or foolish.

M

magic /mædʒɪk/ - (N) Magic is the power to use supernatural forces to make impossible things happen, such as making people disappear or controlling events in nature.

magnet /mægnɪt/ - (magnets) (N) A magnet is a piece of iron or other material which attracts iron toward it.

Master of the Revels /mæstər əv ðə rɛvəlz/ - (N) The Master of the Revels is responsible for looking over the royal events and festivities.

mermaid /mɜrmeɪd/ - (mermaids) (N) In fairy tales and legends, a mermaid is a woman with a fish's tail instead of legs who lives in the sea.

monster /mɒnstər/ - (monsters) (N) A monster is a creature that looks very ugly and frightening.

moonbeam /munbim/ - (moonbeams) (N) A moonbeam is a ray of light from the moon.

moonlight /munlaɪt/ - (N) Moonlight is the natural light that comes from the moon.

murder /mɜrdər/ - (murders, murdered, murdering) (V) To murder someone means to commit the crime of killing them deliberately.

murderer /mɜrdərər/ (murderers) (N) A murderer is a person who commits the crime of killing someone.

N

nest /nɛst/ - (nests) (N) A nest is the home of a bird or other small creature.

nightmare /naɪtmɛər/ - (nightmares) (N) A nightmare is a very frightening dream.

noble /noubəl/ - (nobler, noblest) (ADJ) Noble means belonging to a high social class and having a title.

nun /nʌn/ - (nuns) (N) A nun is a member of a female religious community.

O

obey /oubeɪ/ - (obeys, obeying, obeyed) (V) If you obey a person, a command, or an instruction, you do what you are told to do.

odious /oudiəs/ - (ADJ) If something is odious, it causes hate or extreme dislike.

odor /oudər/ - (N) An odor is a smell.

onstage /ɒnsteɪdʒ/ - (ADV) When an actor or an object is onstage, it means they are on a stage in front of the audience.

out of sight /aut ɒv saɪt/ - (PHRASE) If someone or something is out of sight, they cannot be seen by anyone else.

P

page /peɪdʒ/ - (pages) (N) A page is a young attendant who does small jobs or other duties for a master.

palace /pælɪs/ - (palaces) (N) A palace is a very large impressive house, especially the official home of a king, queen, or president.

pay for something /peɪ fər sʌmθɪŋ/ - (PHRASE) If you are "paying for" an action, it means you are dealing with the consequences that are a result of something you've done.

perform /pərfɔrm/ - (performs, performing, performed) (V) To perform a play, a piece of music, or a dance means to do it in front of an audience.

performance /pərfɔrməns/ - (performances) (N) A performance involves entertaining an audience by singing, dancing, or acting.

permission /pərmɪʃən/ - (N) If you give someone permission to do something, you tell them that they can do it.

point of view /pɔɪnt ɒv vyu/ - (points of view) (N) If you consider something from a particular point of view, you use one aspect of a situation in order to judge it.

R

rage /reɪdʒ/ - (N) Rage is strong anger that is difficult to control.

raise /reɪz/ - (raises, raising, raised) (V) To raise children means to takes care of them until they are grown up.

reason /rizən/ - 1. (reasons) (N) The reason for something is a fact or situation which explains why it happens. 2. (N) The ability that people have to think and to make sensible judgments can be referred to as reason.

refuse /rɪfyuz/ - (refuses, refusing, refused) (V) If you refuse to do something, you deliberately do not do it, or you say firmly that you will not do it.

rehearse /rihɜrs/ - (rehearses, rehearsing, rehearsed) (V) When people rehearse a play, dance, or piece of music, they practice it.

reject /rɪdʒɛkt/ - (rejects, rejecting, rejected) (V) If you reject something such as a proposal or a request, you do not accept it or agree to it.

relationship /rɪleɪʃənʃɪp/ - (relationships) (N) A relationship is a close friendship between two people, especially one involving romantic feelings.

rhyme /raɪm/ - (rhymes, rhyming, rhymed) (V) If one word rhymes with another or if two words rhyme, they have a very similar sound.

rot /rɒt/ - (rots, rotting, rotted) (V) When something rots, it becomes softer and is gradually destroyed.

S

self-respect /sɛlf rɪspɛkt/ - (N) Self-respect is a feeling of confidence and pride in your own ability and worth.

sincere /sɪnsɪər/ - (ADJ) If you say that someone is sincere, you approve of them because they really mean the things they say.

sneak /snik/ - (sneaks, sneaking, sneaked) (V) If you sneak somewhere, you go there very quietly on foot, trying to avoid being seen or heard.

spell /spɛl/ - (spells) (N) A spell is a situation in which events are controlled by a magical power.

spirit /spɪrɪt/ - (spirits) (N) A spirit is a ghost or supernatural being.

sprite /spraɪt/ - (sprites) (N) A sprite is an imaginary creature with magical powers. Sprites are also known as fairies or elves.

supernatural force /supərnætʃərəl fɔrs/ - (supernatural forces) (PHRASE) Supernatural creatures, forces, and events are believed by some people to exist or happen, although they are impossible according to scientific laws.

target /tɑrgɪt/ - (targets) (N) A target is something that someone is trying to hit with a weapon or other object.

taste /teɪst/ - (N) A person with taste is able to make good decisions about things that are attractive and elegant.

temple /tɛmpᵊl/ - (temples) (N) A temple is a building used for the worship of a god or gods.

tyrant /taɪrənt/ - (tyrants) (N) A tyrant is someone who treats the people they have authority over in a cruel and unfair way.

vicious /vɪʃəs/ - (ADJ) A vicious person or a vicious blow is violent and cruel.

vow /vaʊ/ - (vows) (N) A vow is a serious promise or decision to do a particular thing.

William Shakespeare

(ca. 1564–1616 A.D.)

© National Portrait Gallery, London

Many people believe that William Shakespeare was the world's greatest writer in the English language.

The actual date of Shakespeare's birth is unknown. Most people accept that he was born on April 23, 1564. Records tell us that he died on the same date in 1616 at the age of 52.

Shakespeare grew up in Stratford-upon-Avon, a small English village. He was the oldest son of John Shakespeare and Mary Arden, and the third of eight children. The Shakespeares were a well-respected family. John Shakespeare, a tradesman who made gloves and traded leather, became the mayor of the town a few years after Shakespeare was born.

As a child, Shakespeare went to the local schools, where he learned to read and write. Eventually, he also studied Latin and English literature. In 1582, when Shakespeare was 18, he married Anne Hathaway. Hathaway, who was eight years older than Shakespeare, was the daughter of a local farmer. They had three children: Susanna, born on May 26, 1583, and twins, Hamnet and Judith, born on February 2, 1585. Hamnet died from the bubonic plague in 1596.

In 1587, Shakespeare moved to London to be an actor and playwright. His wife and children stayed in Stratford-upon-Avon. Although Shakespeare performed in many plays, it was his playwriting that got the most attention. He soon became famous throughout England. When Queen Elizabeth I died in 1603, her cousin James became king. Shakespeare's acting company often performed for James I. In return, the king allowed Shakespeare's acting company to be called The King's Men.

Shakespeare wrote 38 plays, 154 sonnets, and many poems between 1590 and 1613. No one has ever found any of Shakespeare's original scripts. This makes it difficult to know exactly when each play was written. It was common for plays to change constantly as they were performed. Shakespeare wrote the script and then made changes with each performance. The plays we know today come from written copies taken from different stages of each play. Because of this, there are different versions of many of Shakespeare's plays.

In 1599, Shakespeare's acting company built the Globe Theatre, one of the largest theaters in England. Thousands of people crammed into the theater for each performance. In 1613, the theater burned down. Although the theater was rebuilt in 1614, Shakespeare stopped writing and left London. He returned to Stratford-upon-Avon to live with his family. He died just three years later.

The cause of Shakespeare's death is not known. He was buried at the Church of the Holy Trinity in Stratford-upon-Avon. The words written on his gravestone are believed to have been written by Shakespeare himself:

Good friend for Jesus' sake forbear
To dig the dust enclosed here!
Blessed be the man that spares
*   these stones,*
And cursed be he that moves my bones.

In his will, Shakespeare left most of his possessions to his older daughter, Susanna. The only thing he left to his wife was his "second best bed." Nobody knows what this gift meant.

Shakespeare's last direct descendant, a granddaughter named Elizabeth, died in 1670.

Shakespeare Birthplace Trust

The house that Shakespeare was born and raised in still exists in Stratford-upon-Avon. It is owned and taken care of by the Shakespeare Birthplace Trust. The Trust also cares for these places:

- Mary Arden's Farm: This is the childhood home of Shakespeare's mother.
- Anne Hathaway's Cottage: This is the childhood home of Shakespeare's wife. This is where Shakespeare wooed Anne.
- Hall's Croft: This is the home of Shakespeare's oldest daughter, Susanna.
- Nash's House and New Place: This is the home of Shakespeare's granddaughter Elizabeth Hall. And, this is the site of Shakespeare's last home. He died there in 1616.

Shakespeare's birthplace in Stratford-upon-Avon.

www.shakespeare.org.uk

Martin Droeshout's engraving of Shakespeare

The Trust was started in 1847. It was formed to promote Shakespeare around the world. In 2009, the Trust announced that it had found a new portrait of Shakespeare. The Trust believes that it was painted while Shakespeare was alive.

Martin Droeshout's engraving of Shakespeare (left) appears on the cover of the First Folio of 1623. People who helped publish the First Folio would have known Shakespeare personally. Therefore, the engraving is accepted to be what Shakespeare actually looked like. The new portrait of Shakespeare was once owned by Henry Wriothesley, a loyal supporter of Shakespeare. The portrait is so similar to Droeshout's engraving that it is now suspected to be Droeshout's source.

www.shakespearefound.org.uk

History of A Midsummer Night's Dream

A Midsummer Night's Dream was a successful play for Shakespeare. The first printed edition was made in 1600. Some believe that the play was written to be performed at a wedding. But, little evidence exists to support this idea, and it is not even know if the play was ever performed for any wedding celebration.

It is difficult to know the exact date of when Shakespeare wrote any of his plays. Certain references in A Midsummer Night's Dream lead experts to believe it was written in 1595–6, just before Shakespeare finished writing Romeo and Juliet. Both plays have a stubborn father trying to force his daughter to marry someone she doesn't love. A Midsummer Night's Dream was definitely written while Elizabeth I (1533–1603) was queen. Shakespeare even refers to her in Act II, Scene I (p. 35), where Oberon remembers

when he saw Cupid aiming his arrow at a lovely queen. The arrow misses the queen and hits a flower instead. Shakespeare's connection to the monarchy became stronger when James I became king. Records show that the play was performed in court in 1604, almost ten years after it was written.

Today, A Midsummer Night's Dream is still very popular and has been performed a countless number of times. As much as the play is loved today, some people have never liked it. Samuel Pepys saw a performance of it in 1662 and wrote about it in his journal. He described it as "the most insipid, ridiculous play that I ever saw in my life." Pepys had similar thoughts about a performance of Romeo and Juliet that same year. Either Pepys went to poor performances for both of these plays, or he just didn't like Shakespeare's plays.

Time and Place

The title of A Midsummer Night's Dream is a little misleading. Midsummer is another name for summer solstice, or when the sun is as its highest due to the angle of the earth's axis to the sun. Today this is recognized as occurring on June 21 in the northern hemisphere, and on December 21 in the southern hemisphere. In Shakespeare's time, it was thought to be on June 24. The only time the date is mentioned is in Act IV, Scene I (p. 100), when Theseus guesses that the young couples were in the forest to celebrate May Day. That would make the date May 1. If Theseus is right about the date, midsummer must refer to "midsummer madness," or crazy behavior that can happen at any time.

As for the time period, legend has it that Theseus lived before the Trojan Wars. That means the play would have to be set around 1250 BC. But, the play seems like it takes place much later than that. It seems like the action occurs during Shakespeare's lifetime.

The location is also strange. The characters are from Athens, Greece, but the woodland setting looks just like the English countryside where Shakespeare was raised. Shakespeare was not concerned with making sure the setting matched the real Greece. He placed his characters in a setting that would be familiar to the audience he was entertaining. These "mistakes" somehow add magic to the play.

"The Knight's Tale" from Chaucer's *Canterbury Tales*. In "The Knight's Tale," Theseus, the Duke of Athens, wins the heart of Ipolita, the Queen of the Amazons. This is mentioned in Act I, Scene I (p. 8). The names of Philostrate and Egeus are also taken from this source.

In Act II, Scene I, the mischievous Puck is introduced to the audience as Robin Goodfellow and Hobgoblin (p. 28). Both these names appear in a 1584 publication, *The Discoverie of Witchcraft* by Reginald Scot. In this book, Scot explains how people would leave clothes, milk, and bread out for the spirit known as Robin Goodfellow or Hobgoblin. These treats would stop the spirit from playing tricks on them. This character was used to threaten children in order to get them to behave.

One of the most humorous parts of the play is when Bottom's head turns into a donkey's head. The comedy is found in the beautiful Titania falling in love with this ugly man-beast. Shakespeare took this idea from a 1566 translation of a second-century Latin story, *Transformations of Lucius or The Golden Ass*. In this story, a man is turned into a donkey and a lovely woman

falls in love with him. Interestingly, though, there is a line in Scot's *The Discoverie of Witchcraft* that must have inspired Shakepeare:

If I affirme, that with certeine charmes and popish praiers I can set an horsse or an asses head upon a mans shoulders, I shall not be believed; or if I doo it, I shall be thought a witch.

Regardless of what Pepys said in 1662, *A Midsummer Night's Dream* remains one of Shakespeare's most popular plays. It is the most-performed play in theaters around the world—the perfect entertainment for a warm summer evening.

Sources

Unlike many of Shakespeare's other plays, *A Midsummer Night's Dream* is not adapted from one prior work. Instead, he used many sources and took bits and pieces from others in order to form a new story.

One major source was Ovid's *Metamorphoses*. Shakespeare probably studied this book when he was in school. *Metamorphoses* tries to explain nature as the result of mythical events between gods, goddess, and humans. Similarly, in Act II, Scene I, Titania explains how bad weather is the result of the disagreement between her and Oberon (p. 32). The name *Titania* is from *Metamorphoses*, but Shakespeare is the one who first gives that name to the Fairy Queen.

The story of Pyramus and Thisbe comes from *Metamorphoses* also. In the book, Pyramus's blood makes the mulberry trees dark red. The amateur production of this story in Act V, Scene I (pp. 113–126) might be Shakespeare making fun of a poor adaptation of the story by Arthur Golding in 1567. Theseus and Hippolyta come from another source. That story is found in